saying yes to life
(EVEN THE HARD PARTS)

EZRA BAYDA
with Josh Bartok

Foreword by Thomas Moore

WISDOM PUBLICATIONS · BOSTON

Wisdom Publications
199 Elm Street
Somerville, MA 02144 USA
www.wisdompubs.org

Library of Congress Cataloging-in-Publication Data
Bayda, Ezra.
  Saying yes to life (even the hard parts) / Ezra Bayda with Josh Bartok ;
foreword by Thomas Moore.—1st ed.
     p. cm.
  Includes bibliographical references and index.
  ISBN 0-86171-274-9 (pbk. : alk. paper)
  1. Spiritual life—Zen Buddhism. I. Bartok, Josh. II. Title.
  BQ9288.B395 2005
  294.3'444—dc22
                         2005010440

First Edition
09 08 07 06 05
5   4   3   2   1

Cover design by Laura Shaw
Interior design by Gopa & Ted2, Inc. Set in NeutraText 11/17.5

Wisdom Publications' books are printed on acid-free paper and meet the
guidelines for permanence and durability set by the Committee on Produc-
tion Guidelines for Book Longevity of the Council on Library Resources.

Printed in Canada.
4LR-JB

SAYING YES TO LIFE

(EVEN THE HARD PARTS)

foreword

Many wonderful themes fill these pages: not waiting for your life to be "right" before feeling good about it; loving life when it seems to be a mess and not just when it's going smoothly; opening fully to the unwanted; and recognizing that in fact you can't be fully happy **until** life is difficult.

These paradoxes warm my heart. They cut through the sentimentality that often passes for spiritual insight. They allow you to live **now** rather than some imaginary later when things have been sorted out. Things will never be sorted out. They will never be "right." **You** will never be "right."

This is a tough book. It doesn't let you get away with much. Like all good Zen writing, it pulls the rug out from under your most cherished truths and habits. It makes you question exactly what you thought was beyond question. It shows the paradoxes that rule from minute to minute as you try to get along and make sense of life. And it cleans the slate so you can go on with life freed of all the precious wisdom you have accumulated.

Zen has been an important influence on me for most of my life. It has helped me, a Catholic at heart, to not be attached to my beliefs or my heresies. It has helped me, a trained psychotherapist, to not believe I necessarily know what is going on or what is best for myself or for anyone. It has helped me, as neurotic a person as you might ever expect to meet, to love my life.

Some of the more challenging ideas presented in this book can almost be described as **counter**-inspirational. Yet when I turn them around in my mind, I find something valuable, even necessary. What's more, I am called to question my own versions of the truth—just as I question the ones in this book.

I like this book, not in spite of my questions, but because of them. I like Ezra Bayda because I don't think he assumes he gets it all right. I can't bear writers who understand everything and tell us exactly how to do it all. This book is more like life. You can live with it like a friend or a spouse—not in absolute harmony but in real engagement.

I already have my favorite pages, sayings I don't want to forget, formulations that are clearly inspired. How many books give you that much? This one is surely worth reading. And it's presented in tidy morsels, in pieces you can chew and swallow one at a time. There is a certain outrageousness about this book that gives it life. I don't recommend using it as a means for falling asleep. But I don't want to make too much of the idea of waking up, either.

—Thomas Moore

preface

O NE OF THE AXIOMS of this book is that we need to stop playing it safe. Only then can we recognize what lies at the very heart of all spiritual practice: that the path to true satisfaction entails the willingness to step into unfamiliar territory. Walking the path to becoming truly and fully human requires acknowledging our own edge—that place beyond which we don't want to go—and then learning what it takes to welcome that hard place, to say yes to it—difficulties and all. Saying yes to life—all of it—is realizing that our true identity knows no bounds. This is the only path to lasting joy.

Yet it's all too easy to stray from the genuine path by focusing only on reading and talking about it. We may even start to mistake the things we know intellectually—about wisdom, about compassion, about spiritual practice—for the realities themselves. But in truth, the only things we truly know are those things that we've learned through our own conscious living. And the things we know best are the ones we've learned by working with our difficulties.

Yet sometimes a particular idea, a succinct phrase, can help us clarify what we're right on the brink of seeing. Or it can remind us of something important we've somehow forgotten. The aphorisms and short essays in this book are offered in this spirit.

You can approach this book in different ways. You may wish to read this book in sequence, exploring the particular development that we've presented. Or you might choose to read the book in a less structured way, flipping around and seeing what leaps out. You might try picking one aphorism that you particularly resonate with and using it as a guiding maxim for a day. Or you could copy down one of the aphorisms you find particularly challenging and post it at work or on your refrigerator.

But however you choose to read this book, don't **consume** it. Don't use it to add to your store of knowledge, your supply of wise words. When an individual aphorism or the idea at the heart of one of the essays jumps out at you—**stop**. Pause, perhaps even close the book, and let what you've rediscovered settle in. Test its truth by taking it with you as you go through your day. Let it seep into the very fabric of your life—and let yourself become who you truly are.

—Ezra Bayda

essay titles

saying yes to life
(EVEN THE HARD PARTS)

True happiness has no cause. It is the natural state of our being, when unobstructed.

3

Look carefully! Look without filters and see through your thoughts.

Behind attachments is freedom. Behind fear, love. Behind desire, the quiet joy of being.

What happens when we slow down and pay attention? Everything! Innumerable delights are right at hand.

*Thank **every one** of the ten thousand things: gratitude turns our world right-side-up.*

Though the heart may feel small, it is spacious beyond the mind's imagination.

The spaciousness of the heart can hold the suffering of the world.

the human dilemma

We all have disappointments, fears, inadequacies. And so we build walls—of self-image, of habit, of pretense—to keep these unwanted feelings out, to protect us from feeling them. But in hiding behind these walls, we cut ourselves off from the heart, and the heart from the world. Even so, our disappointments, fears, and inadequacies remain. The question is not whether we can fend these things off forever—we can't. The real question is what we can learn from willingly facing the things we haven't wanted to see. Cowering safely behind our walls, we don't realize the extent of our blind spots, and we can't see the havoc we create with the blind actions that come out of them. Only by letting these walls be dismantled—and thereby realizing the extent to which we are driven by the vanity of our endeavors, the smallness of our attachments, and the urgency of aversion—can we reconnect with the heart.

Real prayer surrenders to the moment. Real prayer listens deeply. Real prayer opens to life.

Learn to pray without ceasing.

the energy for awakening

The energy necessary to awaken constantly leaks away from us, morning till night. As we struggle to hold our lives together—trying to win, trying to please, trying to hide, trying to avoid discomfort—our energy is dissipated in mindless chatter, needless action, wanton daydreams. We rage, we lust, we fear. We gossip, complain, dramatize; we fidget, tense, strain; we fantasize and worry. Above all we try to plan for the unknowable. And all the while the very energy that could fuel our awakening leaks away, drop by drop. Our task is to learn to stop these leaks.

We can see the face of God in everyone and everything by bringing a gentle awareness to the heart that's still too closed to see.

Residing fully in the present moment allows the unconditioned energy of life to flow through the conditioned body and mind.

The willingness to simply rest in the physical experience of your life is the key to spiritual transformation.

Shining the light of awareness transforms that which is observed.

self-observation

We awaken to self-knowledge through the relentless practice of self-observation. Self-observation is not analysis; it
is simply noticing what we think, how we think, what we
fear, how we react, and what our strategies of behavior
are. Notice, notice, notice. In observing ourselves objec-
tively—that is, without judgment—we can begin to see
clearly our fear-based ideas of how we're supposed to be,
how others are supposed to be, how life is supposed to
be. In seeing through our beliefs, we penetrate the count-
less layers of illusions that silently run our lives.

Self-image and social conditions shift like sand; a life built on such a base will never be stable. Awakening to the vast ground of our true nature is the only secure foundation.

When we require that people be different, we block the possibility of real connection with them.

You don't have to get rid of any feelings. You don't need a different personality. Just give up your opinions and self-judgments.

Letting life just be requires mercy toward ourselves.

ideals

As much as we deny it, we still believe we're supposed to be perfect. Our ongoing anxiety and sense of inadequacy testify eloquently to this unexamined truth. In spiritual practice, this trap takes the form of making one attempt after another to measure up to some ideal of how a spiritual practitioner is supposed to be—more calm, loving, wise, or simply more together. Yet becoming truly calm and loving requires that we first see clearly the extent we still punish ourselves by clinging to ideals of perfection.

Love is the wanting to give with no thought of getting.

Give yourself to others, like a white bird in the snow.

When our plans crumble and there seems to be nothing left, it is only by completely surrendering to what is that we can realize that what is left is more than enough.

Suffering is the most effective vehicle for awakening the heart.

judgment

We all make judgments about who we are and how life is, and these judgments become lenses that distort everything we see. We then look through our filtering lens seeking proof that our judgments were right all along. If we think "I'll never measure up," we'll search until we find some "fault" to confirm that this is the truth. But in mistaking our judging thoughts for Truth we miss reality. The devastating power of judgments such as "I can't do it" or "I'm no good" derives from the fact that we never question their verity.

Good fortune is arbitrary, and certainly nothing we can rely on—yet we still cling to the belief that it's our right that things always go our way.

Clinging to notions of how life ought to be, of what you want, of what you hate, always leads to suffering.

discomfort

Perhaps it's the belief that we shouldn't have any problems, any discomfort, any pain, that makes modern life seem so distressing. Life doesn't match our image of how it should be, and we conclude life itself is wrong. We relate to everything from the narrow, fearful perspective of "I want"—and what we want is to feel good. When our emotional distress does not feel good, we recoil from it. The resulting discomfort generates fear, then fear creates even more distress, and distress becomes our enemy, something to be rid of. Let us instead examine our basic requirement that life **should** be comfortable. This one assumption causes all of us endless difficulties.

Most of the time we cruise through life on automatic pilot, gliding across the thin ice of denial. But ignoring the things we don't want to face will not prevent us from falling into the frigid water below.

There is often a vague sense of danger with which we greet almost every person and every situation. If it had a voice, it might whisper, "Please don't hurt me."

Becoming aware of how often we relate from self-protection is a step out of the prison of fear.

No matter how you may be feeling, simply sit down, experience the texture of what is happening in your body and mind—and then just let it be.

meditation

Sitting in meditation allows the body and mind to settle
into stillness. In that stillness we become the openness
that allows all of life in, including the parts we've never
wanted to face. As much as we would like to have pleasing and special experiences, the path of meditation is
about being ever awake—to **whatever** we feel, special or
not. Meditation is not about achieving nice states of mind
while sitting on a cushion. The essence of meditation is to
simply be here, bringing full awareness to just this moment.
When stillness yields to the incessant outpouring of our
overactive brain—we come back again and again to what is,
to awareness of the breath, the body, the environment.

The basic paradox: everything is a mess yet all
is well.

Our nature is connectedness and love—
not the separateness to which our suffering
clings.

When we cling to fear and shame, we forsake
the gratitude of living from our natural being.

The path to love requires open-hearted attention to the very things that seem to block our way to it.

transformation

The basic pain of feeling separate and disconnected is a fundamental human experience. Yet when we consciously reside in the physical feeling of separation, we come closer to recognizing its insubstantiality. Continually bringing the light of awareness to our viscerally held beliefs, our pretenses, our protections, our anxieties, begins to dissolve these self-imposed boundaries, the boundaries that block awareness of the vast reality of being. This is the slow, transformative path to freedom.

Saying yes to life means saying yes to everything, even longing, fear, and pain.

Joy is impossible without pain.

It's the heart's nature to give.

Giving from "should" is not giving from the heart.

Spiritual work is possible in one place alone: here, in exactly what you are experiencing right now.

"what is this?"

We can't wake up simply by wishing to. Without specific, ongoing effort we will continue to sleepwalk through our self-centered dream. Genuine awakening requires bringing attention repeatedly to the present moment of our life. One laserlike tool to help us do this is the practice of continually asking ourselves, "What is this?" Used in this way, the question becomes a **koan**, and as with all koans, the "answer" can never be conceptual. Don't try to analyze what the moment is **about**. Instead, fully feel the texture of what your life **truly is** right now. The only real answer to the question "What is this?" is your immediate experience itself.

The Zen mind speaks with strength, saying "Just do it!"

The Zen heart speaks softly, saying "Just let it be."

Living from perceived boundaries creates imaginary prisons.

Be who you truly are—not who you think
you are or believe you should be.

It's not necessary to connect with the stars to go beyond our own boundaries. We can realize increased awareness in smaller steps: hearing the song of a bird, looking into the eyes of a newborn, sharing another's pain.

Every event is an opportunity to connect with the vastness of being.

39

When our self-imposed prison walls come down, all that remains is the connectedness that we are.

emotions

Experiencing our emotions fully, without wallowing in them or turning away, allows us to break through the layers of protective armor and connect with the heart. Fully felt, our emotions can clear the path to the deep well of compassionate love that is the essence of our being. From the wider perspective of the witness, the limited sense of "self"—coiled tightly around unwanted emotions—begins to expand. We then see this "self" for what it is: a complex of deeply held beliefs, physical sensations, and distant memories. And we are free to receive all the world.

Peace is found not through seeking peace, but through residing completely in what is.

You believe your opinions; you believe your judgments; you believe your emotions. And these beliefs become your ego—but this ego is not you.

43

Time is fleeting: don't hold back your heart.

anger

What holds us back from living open-heartedly? What shuts life out? What cuts off our natural ability to truly love? As much as anything, the answer is this: our anger. Though our anger hurts both ourselves and others, we still cling to it. When our expectations or desires aren't met, anger insists, "No, I won't accept this!" Yet even as we feel the pain that comes from rejecting things that can't be changed, we continue to indulge in anger's aversion with a stubbornness that defies all sense.

Look deeply: the seemingly solid "I" is really many "me's"—and what's more, they often disagree!

Effort is necessary in spiritual practice;
strain is not.

Confusion is a state out of which nothing but confusion comes. Often the real source of confusion is that we don't know who we are.

Clarity comes from staying present with the physical experience of confusion itself— without replaying the confused thoughts.

What is the path? Residing in this very life, exactly as it is right now ... liking or not liking has nothing to do with it.

Opening fully to the unwanted is the key to living with appreciation.

anger as practice

Do you imagine anger should be suppressed? Pushing anger down, below awareness, does not free us from its grip. When we do this, anger festers, and its consequences continue unabated. Whether suppressed anger resurfaces as physical symptoms, depression, passive aggression, or explosive rage—sooner or later it will rise. Yet expressing anger in words and actions is no more skillful than pushing it down. And when we justify our anger, we get hijacked into believing that our thoughts are The Truth. Without justifying anger, repressing it, or acting on it, we have only to genuinely feel our anger. When we do, we see the present moment of anger is very quiet—and also very specific. Anger is never just ANGER—which is a mental concept. Rather it is a concrete, visceral experience—perhaps of tightness, pulsing, heat, pressure—plus strongly believed thoughts. Bringing attention to these sensations in the quiet light of awareness, you may experience a release from the constricting belief that this emotion is "you."

Spiritual practice is not about a special technique, such as meditation, or about feeling a special way, such as calm or centered. It is about living increasingly awake.

Your "true nature" includes everything, even the parts of yourself you don't like.

Everything that happens offers an opportunity to awaken.

Desire and fear are the principal causes of the mind's endless agitation.

saying yes to fear

Everyone feels fear. But giving in to fear is what makes our lives narrow and dark. Fear-based action is the source of all conflict; fearful response, the root of all sorrow. Fear is what prevents intimacy and undermines love. But we're often not aware of how fear drives so much of what we do. There is often fear behind what we call kindness, fear in ambition, in depression, and always fear in anger. Every time we give in to fear we lose our life. In fear we imagine a terrible future, and in this imagining we create a terrible present. We bring upon ourselves the very misery that we are desperately trying to push away. The secret to living with fearful feelings is saying **yes** to the objects of fear—not being swallowed by them, but welcoming them as invitations to move toward freedom.

We cling to our beliefs, even when we know they cause us suffering. We maintain our illusions, even when they make us miserable. We know this, but we refuse to act on it.

What are we waiting for?

Rarely do we experience the presence born of knowing who we really are and what we are doing on this earth. Realizing how rarely we're present to life is itself a crucial step in awakening.

Without the intention to awaken, there can only be sleep.

Stay alert to the easy shift from the illusions of false expectations to the illusions of anger and fear that follow in their wake.

illusions

In the honeymoon stage of any spiritual practice, everything seems so fresh and mysterious. But as the lustrous sheen of novelty wears thin, as disappointments accrue, as old illusions are uncovered, practice will predictably and inevitably seem to become dry. The discouraging conclusions we draw in this dry place may seem like underlying truths, but they are just **new** illusions arising from an ever-changing and natural process. Becoming literally "disillusioned"—disabused of our own illusory notions—is always a good thing, a sure sign that your spiritual practice is proceeding apace. Disillusionment with practice is not a problem. The problem arises when we replace one illusion with another.

How can we experience satisfaction and appreciation when we spend so much time lost in the mental world—literally addicted to our thoughts?

Knowledge alone can never heal the wound of being. Only by being fully present is our intrinsic wholeness revealed.

Clear mind does not arise from thinking clearly. Clear mind is what remains when you're not caught by thoughts.

Spiritual practice has very little to do with explanations.

the world of why

When difficulties arise, one of our first reactions is to ask "Why?" We want certainty, logic, simple causality. We think this kind of knowing is necessary to alleviate our discomfort. Yet, most often, the reasons we come up with to explain why we think and behave the way we do are at best only marginally accurate. In reality, everything affects everything else, everything relates to everything else. The complexity of this interrelatedness defies description, and our subjective filters make explanation even more dubious. Yet we still look for simple explanations to account for what we see, unaware of the blinders obscuring our vision. Deep understanding never lies in the cognitive world of **why**, but in directly experiencing the ambiguous complexity of the present moment.

Simply sitting, doing nothing—nothing is excluded.

Grasping after happiness doesn't bring happiness; it only perpetuates the grasping mind.

Cease grasping and happiness becomes possible.

All your ego-based suffering is just a complex of believed thoughts and unpleasant sensations.

no one to be

As we relentlessly observe ourselves, the images we have of who we are and who we need to be—which at one time seemed so real—begin to peel away like layers of an onion. Pleasant self-images may give way to uglier ones, each seeming equally real until that layer too peels away. As every illusory idea of who we are is stripped off, we can finally experience the quivering freedom of not needing to be anyone at all.

Looking with a mind that's awake reveals the shimmering pulse of life. Looking with a mind full of thoughts reveals only your thoughts.

That we are all one does not mean we are all the same.

To truly awaken is to experience oneness in the world of difference.

This experience right now—**whatever** it is—is the doorway to reality. If we try to avoid the mundane or if we seek out the special, we bolt this door.

rituals and reality

Rituals and forms in spiritual practice can be useful, but in themselves they have little to do with seeing the truth. We must question whether we use the forms and rituals to connect with what is, or as a way to hide in familiar security. The longer one practices in a particular tradition, the easier it becomes to hide in the routines, in doing it "right," and—especially—in the jargon. Thus we trap ourselves in the protected cocoon of comforting predictability, unable to experience the reality of what our life really is.

We wander as if through a dark tunnel looking for illumination, yet the light of awareness is always at hand.

The only path of the truly human being is to awaken to who we really are.

On the spiritual path none of us is separate,
and each of us must do our own work.

Using meditation like a drug to treat the symptoms of fear will never make you free of their cause.

meditation as detour

Until you practice with the messy, unromantic, ordinary ups and downs of everyday life, any efforts to "feel calm" while sitting on a cushion will be no more than a temporary detour from the truth of your life. What good is it to have nice experiences during meditation, then shortly after speak contemptuously because you don't know your own anger? Beware of using meditation to bypass your life's difficulties.

Believing you're a "good meditator" doesn't foster good meditation; it only bolsters another deluded self-image.

Pursuing your fantasy of enlightenment is often driven by the same greed and ambition you seek to dispel.

Are you still caught in the dream of an "enlightened" experience that will leave you permanently clear and peaceful?

One step toward awakening: drop the story-line of "me."

goals

We set goals that we think will guide us through the course of life. But we forget that our goals are not so much conscious choices as they are aggregates of our innate disposition, our particular conditioning, and ever-changing life circumstances. To think that we can will our destiny is a false prop, the vanity of needing to see ourselves as the agent of change.

We have problems, but we don't want problems—and that's the problem!

Suffering is guaranteed as long as we demand that life be free from discomfort.

You believe you can't be happy because your life is difficult. This is backwards. You can't be truly happy **until** your life is difficult.

Anxiety is always about the future. Bring your mind to the present, to what is happening right now, and you can recognize anxiety as just another thought.

*See your thoughts for what they are: just thoughts. And see them for what they **aren't**: the truth about who you are and what life is.*

Realize that the feeling that we need fixing is predicated on the belief that we are broken. That belief is just another thought.

Notice how often thinking and talking are detours from the painful work of being present to life.

Suffering is the result of insisting that something be other than it is.

In every moment, you have a choice: to live the life of spiritual practice or retreat into comfort and security.

resistance

Resistance is a conditioned response of the ego; it's the ego's effort to maintain control, the ego's fear of giving up the known. Often our resistance prevents us from staying in the present moment for more than a few seconds. We resist because we want to avoid feeling the underlying jangle of our actual experience. We move away from discomfort, into the false comfort of our thoughts. But no matter what form it takes, resistance brings no peace; we strengthen whatever we resist. By resisting something we solidify it, empowering it to stay in our life.

Your difficulties are not obstacles on the spiritual path, they **are** the path.

perseverance

Our efforts in practice will inevitably "fail." We will have periods of aspiration and effort, followed by periods of resistance and apathy. Ups and downs in practice are predictable and inevitable. The countermeasure is always to simply persevere.

Attend to one more breath, notice one more thought, experience one more sensation— again and again and again.

Notice your ideals and expectations. Watch your habitual patterns. Observe your emotional reactions. See them for what they are. This is the path to transformation.

The little self, driven by fear and a craving for comfort, identifies only with "me." The true self, driven by nothing, identifies with the unbounded awareness that we truly are.

fear

Fear tells us to stop, to stay within the boundary of our protected cocoon-world. Yet when we feel fear, if we take even one small step toward it rather than yielding to our habitual pulling away, we move one step closer to the vast mind that lies beyond. When we feel fear, instead of saying "I'm afraid," thus reinforcing our identification with our fear as who we are, we can simply say, "Fear is present." Thus fear's power gradually dissipates, and we begin to free ourselves from it. When we simply experience fear just as it is—without our opinions, judgments, and reactions—fear is not nearly so frightening.

When life presents difficulties we can crumble or we can learn. Aspiring to be free tips the scale toward learning.

The willingness to open to life's difficulties does not depend on liking them.

Discipline is essential—but it can all too easily become stoic, militant, even grim.

Spiritual work is serious—but not somber.

Compassion isn't just offering kind words.
Compassion is offering your very being.

fear in others

In some people anxiety is obvious. Others may appear calm and at ease with life, yet still be scared to death—of intimacy, of criticism, of loss, of **something**. Just because fear in others is not obvious doesn't mean it's not there. The fear may be hidden, but it is just as powerful and just as frightening. Recalling this can foster compassion.

In this moment, is your view life-centered or self-centered?

When you grieve over someone's death, is it wholly the loss of the person you're mourning, or in part the loss of your own dreams?

It is absolutely amazing that we can spend our entire life in waking sleep and hardly know it. It's as if we've taken a potion, falling deeply into the self-centered dream. The antidote: a never-ending effort to stay awake.

First ask: "What is going on right now?"
Then ask: "What is spiritual practice in this situation?"

Disappointment is always a reminder that you're still attached to something. Take that disappointment as opportunity to investigate and awaken.

Arrogance toward others often masks contempt for ourselves.

We wonder how people can't see the most obvious things about themselves—yet we forget those people are us!

relating from big mind

When strong emotions arise in the midst of a conflict, it's generally best to keep quiet, to spend some time in meditation. It's certainly better to avoid getting hooked into self-justification and blame—which is what inevitably happens when we open our mouths while gripped by flaring emotion. When we relate to others from our small mind—with all its desires, opinions, and judgments—we relate only to the small mind of the other. And thus we stay caught in a diminished life that guarantees distress. When we relate to another from the big mind—from spacious awareness—we relate to the deepest nature of the other as well. This is the path from conflict to communion.

Experiencing the deepest connection with life often requires taking a step into unknown territory.

A life of equanimity and appreciation is lived in the immediacy of the present—not in the mind.

The future exists nowhere except in our thoughts.

A spiritual teacher is sometimes necessary to help you uncover that one thing you do not wish to see.

students and teachers

To always view authority with suspicion, to believe it's unhealthy to ever submit to another, to see yourself as wholly independent, to believe you are completely free— this is delusion. And this delusion prevents true learning on the spiritual path. But neither can we place spiritual teachers on pedestals, imagining them saintly, finished, above the travails of our daily world. This delusion that the teacher is perfect arises out of the childish mind that still wants to be saved. But spiritual teachers aren't perfect; they too are ongoing processes. In fact, unless teachers continue to work at their own edge, with their own fears and difficulties, they can no longer be effective teachers, because they are no longer connected with others.

A spiritual teacher, no matter how skillful, can teach only in proportion to a student's true willingness to learn.

A true teacher wants nothing more than to see you stand on your own two feet.

Demanding that someone make you feel some special way is a sure recipe for disappointment and conflict.

Truly loving others does not depend on whether they satisfy your needs.

Do you still hold to the false hope that love will magically extinguish all of your relationship difficulties?

Do you still believe the fallacy that love will save you?

relationships

The root cause of most difficulties in relationships is the fact that we want something from another. We imagine that we need the other person to be a certain way. Why? Perhaps so that we ourselves will then feel a certain way— safe, supported, appreciated, happy. When we don't get what we want, when other people don't act the way we wish they would, relationship difficulties begin. We then view these difficulties as impediments to happiness, even obstacles on our spiritual path. But these difficulties— especially in relationships—are themselves our path. While we might **prefer** that a person be a particular way, it is our misguided **requirement** that they be this way that stops real love from flowing. By giving up our requirements of others, we open to the love that already connects us.

Spiritual practice is about increasingly entering into love—not personal love, but the love that is the nature of our being.

Until we face our fears we can never live from love.

what we want from others

The fact that relationships often bring the most painful and unhealed aspects of our life out of the shadows makes them a powerful teacher. Yet who really wants such a teacher? In truth, what we want from relationships is ... **what we want!** The beauty of relationships as spiritual practice is that the disappointment of not getting what we want eventually motivates us to awaken.

Joy's greatest expression is giving ourselves to others.

the spiritual practice of relationships

The spiritual practice of relationships is about working on ourselves only, freeing ourselves from the constricting grip of our own unhappiness. It is not the other person's job to take our unhappiness away; our discomfort is our own responsibility. Attending to our own spiritual tasks—seeing our judgments, opinions, beliefs, demands, and staying present with the fears out of which they all arise—frees others to move toward us. Then, when they no longer feel the need to defend, they become more willing to take care of **their** job. Thus joy in relationships becomes possible.

Spiritual practice includes learning how to open-heartedly receive the shocks of life—the things you don't like, the people who criticize you, the job that goes wrong, the partner that leaves, the health that fails you—whatever shakes you up.

Before we enter the path, we see our experiences in terms of "good" or "bad." Upon truly entering the path, we see them only as opportunities to awaken.

A sense of entitlement guarantees that eventually you will see yourself as a victim.

seeing others

When we first meet people, we inevitably see them through the filters of all our associations, expectations, and projections. Over time, as the filters diminish, we may feel betrayed or deceived: "You're not the person you were when we first met!" Of course they're not—in fact, they never were.

The very beliefs that we hold to be "my deepest truths" are often the ones that should be most suspect.

As the veil of separation begins to part, reality shimmers and the world is seen differently. Then, when the veil has disappeared completely, everything is the same again—but not exactly.

Life's wonder and mystery can be discovered as easily at a traffic light as on a mountaintop.

Addressing the anger and fear that fuel our unkindness allows us to connect with the basic kindness that is the essence of our being.

betrayal

When we feel betrayed, we rarely question the expectations, beliefs, and supposed needs that underlie our feelings. The thought that we've been betrayed arises and we simply believe it—and then fall quickly into anger, blame, and resentment. Yet such sentiments are unfailing reminders that we're stuck in the small mind's requirement that life and people should fit our designs for them. If we're truly committed to spiritual practice, we might even thank the other party for pushing us into fertile fields of practice we would rarely choose to enter on our own.

Strong emotional reactions always signal the need to look more deeply at your beliefs.

There is no magic key that opens the door to truth; yet without perseverance we won't realize that the door has never been locked.

You can enter silence not by trying to enter, but through the constant soft effort to let life be.

You'll never be free from discomfort and fear—yet liberation comes from not **needing** to be free from them.

fundamental security

Ultimately we need to understand that spiritual life isn't about being safe, secure, or comfortable. It's not that we won't sometimes feel secure in the course of our spiritual practice; we surely will. And so too will we sometimes feel insecure. Yet there is a **fundamental security** that develops from many years of practice—though it is a far cry from the immediate comfort we may now crave.

We often look to our relationships to mask an anxious quiver of being that cries out for relief. Yet another person can never heal our anxiety; we can only do that for ourselves. But that doesn't keep us from asking others to do it.

*We think we need to be loved. But we have it backwards. As adults, we don't need to **be loved.** The only real emotional need, if you want to call it that, is **to love.***

Call to mind the deepest, darkest, most negative truth about yourself—and know that this "truth" is a lie.

Only by uncovering and consciously entering the deep hole inside—thereby seeing through the false perception of who we are—can we ultimately reconnect with awareness of our basic wholeness.

Entering your own fear-based pain allows you to begin to relate to the pain of others. And thus you can experience a sense of kinship with humanity.

As we feel the pain that all people feel in facing an uncontrollable world, compassion naturally arises—even for our "enemies."

Contrary to the romantic fantasies we have about relationships, in actuality they often push us directly into our blind longings, our dark fears, and our unhealed pain.

conflict in relationships

The origin of relationship conflict is this: One person, blindly driven by their own perceived and mechanical needs, meets another person equally driven by their own needs. When their needs aren't met they clash, pitting themselves against each other, as if the other were the enemy. Thus, when two people who haven't uncovered their own fear-based drives reach a point of conflict, the result is like a collision of machines. To the extent that we're not aware of our mechanical responses to our conditioning, we're bound to follow this predictable path.

We're often more attached to the **belief** that we need a particular person in order to be happy than we are to the actual person.

There is a never-ending struggle between just being here and our addiction to the false comfort and security of our mental world.

Awakening requires turning away from the constant search for comfort and the endless avoidance of pain.

You can run from your fears or you can live from the heart—the choice is yours.

anger and blame in relationships

All of our defensive maneuvers in relationships, especially our anger and blame, are born out of fear—of rejection, of being alone, of being controlled, of not getting what we want, of intimacy, of inadequacy, of unworthiness. The path to harmonious relationships requires acknowledging and facing these fears. In relationship difficulties, only by being directly present with our core pain—not as a concept, but as a complex of uncomfortable bodily sensations—can we take a step beyond thinking, beyond self-justifying, and beyond the enslavement of our narrow agendas.

Pain is rarely as unbearable as you **think** it is.

Truly healing suffering requires experiencing, in your very cells, the distress that arises when you hold to your requirements that life be other than it is.

Sometimes love means allowing others to learn from their suffering—just as you do from yours—rather than trying to take that suffering away.

empathy in relationships

The more we practice with our own struggles and relate to them as our vehicle to awakening, the less we will judge our struggles as defects. Likewise in relationships: the more we can remember that others also have the wish to learn from their struggles, the less we will judge others as defective when we see them caught in their distress.

Equanimity is being present with **whatever** is happening, without believing your judgments about it.

Awareness is like the open sky, and its contents are like clouds—ever-changing and never as substantial as they appear.

*By identifying with the spaciousness of awareness, it is possible to feel anxiety, yet not **be** anxious.*

We wish for people to accept us as we are, but in so doing we reject them for who they are.

forgiveness

Spiritual practice always entails forgiveness—at least as long as there is even one person we can't forgive. But real forgiveness is not some form of magnanimous acceptance of others "even though they did us wrong." Rather, with true forgiveness we loosen the grip on our treasured resentment. Often the most difficult part of forgiving another is facing the fact that we don't actually **want** to forgive them. Yet the process of forgiveness also requires that we experience, within ourselves, the fact that we are not so different from those we are so ready to judge. Experiencing this shared pain of humanity—the realization that all of us are acting out of protectedness and fear—allows forgiveness to come forth on its own.

Anger brings a sense of strength—but it is a deluded strength that can only cause more suffering.

We love the feeling of being right, but righteously justifying our anger will never lead to true satisfaction.

The beliefs that are most deeply hidden often have the greatest power over us. Their strength dissipates as they are brought into the light of awareness.

Suffering in itself has no merit. Only conscious suffering has value.

Seeing truth may require residing consciously in the doubt that feels all-consuming.

grief

Few circumstances awaken our aspiration to live more directly from the heart than the grave illness or death of a loved one. In such times of naked pain, we're no longer so intent on clinging to our protections, so interested in preserving our small comforts and our fleeting goals. At such times, we may become aware of just how strongly we hold our hearts back in fear. At this point, grief becomes a doorway to enter more deeply into our life.

When you understand that suffering is your teacher, it's no longer the enemy you have to conquer.

Look carefully: sometimes behind the sadness of grief lies, inexplicably, a poignant sense of joy.

We can't avoid grief and the pain of loss—but we can avoid indulging in the melodrama of "me."

Within grief and loss there is always longing—
for wholeness, for harmony, for connection.
Trying to "move on" too quickly denies the
value of inner exploration.

breathing into loss

When facing calamities, we can certainly tell ourselves to "be strong," or comfort ourselves with words about the "mysterious ways" in which the universe works. But invoking these as mere attitudes, without the corresponding inner understanding, is just another way of burying our experience, armoring our heart against fear and pain. When feeling sadness and loss, we can't simply use slogans to surrender to the moment; rather we must actively bring awareness to the physical reality of the situation. By breathing the physical-emotional sensations of loss directly into the center of the chest, we can experience the healing power of the vast and spacious heart. Breathing our loss into the chest undermines the seductive power of tragic thoughts. Even though sadness may remain, it's possible to experience a lightness inside the dark, unencumbered by the weight of our melodramatic scenarios.

"Just let it go" is more a philosophy than an option. If it were possible to "just let go," we'd all know freedom right now. Often our only real choice is to just let it **be**.

152

Don't try to change; just be aware.

Awareness heals.

Fear warns us to close down and defend. The heart calls us to open up and connect.

The belief that fear will always prevail is just another voice of fear, feeding its own preservation.

Fear tells us we have reached an edge beyond which we're unwilling to go. Aspiration tells us to take yet one more step forward.

We dread the helplessness of losing control. Yet freedom lies in recognizing the reality that some things are ever beyond our control—and the only option is to make peace with helplessness itself.

Acting with clarity is always impeded by the negative energy of anger.

Our attachment to having things go a particular way perpetuates a narrow, self-centered life.

Spiritual practice is a mixture of struggle and integration, of confusion and clarity, of discouragement and aspiration, of feeling failure and going deeper.

Don't imagine that the spiritual path is a straight line to a fixed goal.

the pace of change

Expecting an epiphany—some single moment of insight that will forever banish the experience of fear, anger, neediness—may prevent us from noticing the slow and almost imperceptible ways spiritual practice subtly transforms us. With patience and perseverance, our habitual reactive patterns slowly erode, until one day we find ourselves in a situation that had always made us anxious—and we notice the anxiety is simply gone.

When stuck in apathy, procrastination, or the morass of depression, choose one small task and complete it mindfully. Momentum will follow.

Being very busy is often a strategy, a choice.

We must not let it be an **excuse** for how we live.

You don't need to be angry to effect positive change.

efforts and resistance

Whenever we make efforts, the ego will find ways to trick us and divert us from the path. Over time, as this predictable pattern of effort and resistance becomes apparent, we are no longer so easily blindsided by the maneuvers of the ego. Nonetheless, the force of resistance can be strong. The countermeasure is always to persevere in face of the inevitable hindrances and discouragements.

The belief that there is an eternal flow of life beneath the world of appearances may give solace; but it is still just an **idea** within the world of appearances.

Thinking you finally understand awakening will lull you into the deepest sleep of all.

Believing that doing is somehow better than not doing is an error that leads to a compulsion to "fix" ourselves.

Believing that not doing is somehow better than doing is an error that leads to passivity and self-satisfaction.

Dropping your façades, what remains?

Just being.

inside and out

It is only in our thoughts that ideas, beliefs, and problems become solid, dark, and unyielding. Reality itself is moveable, light, ever-changing. In our minds we seem trapped, in reality we are utterly free.

Our self-images define our own boundaries, limiting us to the narrow ideas of who we believe ourselves to be.

Pushing away your "monsters" just makes them more solid. Instead, bring to them the light touch of awareness—for just one more breath—and gradually they'll lose their power.

What are you still pushing away?

Fear of the unknown is the root of violence.

history

We may assume that history is rational, but why should the unfolding of history be any different from the unfolding of our life as we live it—full of the human frailties of ignorance, confusion, and misjudgment? The failure to work with our own inner turmoil—our own wishes for power, our own self-centered desires for acquisition, our fearful greed, and our need to control—results in hatred, intolerance, and aggression. Without inner understanding, individuals as well as societies will continue to flounder, and the social and political chaos we see around us will rage unchecked.

The lack of individual awareness, multiplied throughout society, is the source of all conflicts and all wars.

Trying to change yourself prevents true transformation.

Look closely: your judgments are never really about another; they're always about you!

the addiction of blaming

Blaming is an addiction. Justifying ourselves can keep us lost in our stories for hours, days, and even years. Blaming puts the focus on the perceived faults of the other and lets us evade the necessity of directing our attention inward. Blame always separates, always disconnects. Overcoming addiction to blaming is an absolute prerequisite to experiencing the connectedness that is the essence of who we are.

The first precept in healing conflict in relation-

ships is to refrain from blaming.

Feeling disappointment is a natural part of being human. Festering in resentment is against our deepest nature.

Having preferences is not a problem, nor is enjoying them. But when preferences crystal-lize into requirements, we suffer.

177

Trying to run away from pain guarantees it will follow.

blaming as defense

Blaming is a defense against feeling the anxious quiver of our own experience. When we stop blaming and defending, we're often left with the one thing we least want: the trembling core of pain that we've spent our life trying to avoid. Yet coming face to face with that well of pain is what brings us to the very heart of our life's practice.

You will never make the effort a spiritual life requires as long as you still believe that your present mode of living will bring you genuine satisfaction.

Stop playing it safe by trying to avoid adversity. Act from the heart and let circumstances unfold as they will.

Giving in to fear and anger makes life the enemy.

Confronting the objects of fear, though useful, is not as liberating as changing your relation to fear itself.

181

Inconsolable suffering can console us by making us feel special. But this feeling of specialness diverts us from true freedom.

the heart of suffering

Sometimes when our emotions are particularly intense, nothing we've learned from spiritual practice seems relevant. Isn't it when we become lost in our darkest emotions that we disconnect from the heart and judge ourselves most harshly? In these darkest moments, use the breath as a conduit to bring all the sensations of suffering into the center of the chest. In these moments, breathing even the most chaotic emotion directly into the heart is an act of compassion for ourselves. By opening to our personal core of pain, we open to the universal pain of being human. Though we may fear the pain will destroy us, opening to it connects with that which is truly indestructible.

When you reach the point where you think you can go no farther, taking one more step, one more breath into the heart, is all that's required.

The extent to which we fall "madly in love" is often proportional to the urgency we feel to avoid longing and loneliness.

The willingness to let loneliness just be is the only way to transcend it.

What we want most from another is often most difficult for them to give. Conversely, what's most difficult for us to give is often what another wants most from us.

sex

On some level, we as a society regard sexuality as something dark, forbidden. This shadowy undercurrent of puritanical sentiment still flows deep in our cultural memory. As a consequence, the desire for sex is rarely simple. Sometimes it is imbued with the thrill of conquest or the lure of the forbidden. Often it is driven by the thirsting desire for excitement and romance, to cover over the anxious quiver of our aloneness. And almost always, from our very core, there comes the desperate craving for acceptance, for love. Yet the power of our sexual energy is in itself neither good nor bad. Far more important than the mere denial or fulfillment of desires, the clarity of our awareness determines whether our sexuality is a heaven or hell.

Look carefully: sexual fantasy is often based in the desire to escape the discomfort of longing, neediness, or even boredom.

When desires arise, so does the belief that we **must** *satisfy them. The problem is that belief—not that desire.*

In seeking to be perfect, we are really trying to affirm our imagined imperfection—the angst-driven belief that things will never be right, that **we** will never be right.

Ideals are always detours on the spiritual path.

189

Observing ourselves does not require think-ing, or judging, or analyzing. It only requires observing.

work

We often decide to leave a job when we feel stuck, anxious, or simply unhappy. But on the spiritual path, we can't measure the value of something simply by how much comfort or pleasure it gives us. If you're having a strong emotional reaction to your job, there is always something of spiritual value to be learned there. Our emotional reactions are based on what we bring to the job—our expectations, needs, and agendas—rather than on the job itself. But our real job—our life's job—is to become awake to who we really are, regardless of the situation. By seeing clearly the specifics of our own habitual patterns, and by bringing awareness to the fears out of which these patterns arise, we can move from being overwhelmed by the chaos or tedium of the workplace to being liberated by it.

When we identify with what we do, we lose connection to who we are.

When contemplating what our life's work might be, we are often driven by our attachment to security. Perhaps the one question we don't ask often enough is "What do I have to offer?"

Honesty is living without pretense—realizing that there's no one special we need to be.

Seeing ourselves as the one who can get things done or being attached to the results of what we do will surely lead to frustration, disappointment, and burnout.

Real joy is often just a quiet presence in the moment.

mindfulness at work

There is nothing romantic, mystical, or even exciting about practicing with the mundane activities at work. Nonetheless, applying mindfulness to our daily routines is the blue-collar labor of daily practice. Picking up a ringing phone, opening a door, or even going to the bathroom, can all be reminders to be awake in the moment.

The most basic human fear is the fear of extinction—frequently more of the ego than the physical body.

Don't worry about what happens after the death of the body; pay attention instead to the "deaths within life"—the times when you are closed in anger, in fear, in protective stances, in resisting the unwanted.

Suffering turns into hopelessness when you forget that it's your teacher.

Courage is not about being unafraid. Courage is the willingness to be with fear.

money

Spiritual practice must include everything, even the temporal worldliness of money. We may imagine that, spiritual practitioners that we are, finances are not worthy of our consideration; yet these issues make an especially rich field for practice. Money issues are rarely about money. Observe your beliefs and behaviors around money—try to see them with clarity and precision. Then bring awareness to the well of emotion out of which your beliefs and behaviors arise. You may discover that behind most financial insecurity is the terror of losing control or feeling helpless. Honestly facing this fear is the price we pay to be free.

Many spiritual practitioners hold the perhaps unconscious view that money is somehow impure, yet simultaneously value things only in proportion to what they pay for them.

As painful as it may be to face your deepest fears, realize it's more painful to hide from them.

Until you become intimate with your fears, they will always limit your ability to love.

Of the many pitfalls on the spiritual path, gullibility and suggestibility are the two that are often hardest to see in oneself.

Even spiritual discipline can become just another way to satisfy the need to feel in control.

activity and awareness

The wisdom of Zen is often reduced to "chop wood, carry water"—to simply do what we're doing without unnecessary thinking. But this can be more simplistic than wise. To be immersed in what we're doing does not necessarily mean that we're awake. In fact, being absorbed in activity is often the deepest form of sleep. Being awake in activity means paying attention to the activity, but not in a narrow way, where most of life is shut out. **Fully doing** includes a broader awareness, with a larger sense of presence and clarity of mind.

It is difficult for spiritual practice to truly penetrate the fiber of our being. Without a teacher, this difficulty is compounded enormously.

Whenever you're stuck in distress, penetrate your confusion with this question: What is my most believed thought right now?

Staying open to the groundlessness of not knowing where to turn or what is right is a stepping-stone into clarity and truth.

doing what is right

When faced with situations in which we see a wrong that
needs to be addressed, we may never know with certainty
what is the right thing to do. Nor can we ever fully control
the outcome of our actions. Nonetheless, when we see
such a wrong, as long as the heart is clear of the negativity
of anger, we must do what we perceive is right. With the
humility of uncertainty and the clarity of the wish to do no
harm, we must not hold ourselves back in fear.

Comparing yourself to ideals is just another subtle way of resisting your life as it is.

Our distress, which seems like a very real bar-
rier, is just an artificial prop, which we use to
create the story of "me."

Almost all of our difficulties in relationships come from wanting people to be different than they are.

the need to help

The natural urge to help, to give, to connect, will often be intertwined with more self-centered agendas—wanting to be seen as helpful, wanting to achieve results, needing to be appreciated. If we are attached to being compassionate, if we **need** to be helpful, this will require that we find people who seem helpless, or situations that seem to call for help. This sense of urgency distorts the genuine wish to help and is a clear indicator that we're being motivated by a need to prove our own worth.

Seeing clearly your own unkindness begins to transform it.

When fear arises, often the shame we feel over seeing ourselves as weak magnifies our suffering. Clearly seeing the nature of shame's self-judgment loosens fear's grip over us.

Believing that we "create our own illness" and that with "better" practice we can "defeat" it, is another version of believing in sin and salvation. Sickness, old age, and death are natural parts of life; and pain simply **is**. None of them are sins, enemies, or failings.

We don't need to wage war with ourselves. There is no enemy within.

Health is not the absence of illness; it is the state of being undefeated by illness.

Illness is one more path to becoming whole.

It is natural and even intelligent to have an aversion to pain—but we convert this instinct into suffering by adding our judgments about it.

Fear is neither an enemy nor an obstacle. When you feel fear tightening in your chest, don't try to push it away. Try welcoming it as an opportunity to move toward freedom.

taking a leap

There is a great value in doing new things, not just for diversion or escape, but in order to help us awaken. When we put ourselves in a new or foreign situation, that very act awakens our senses, our awareness, our presence. Sometimes we have to take a leap in order to experience and heal the fear that holds us ever at the edge of familiar safety. Our task in awakening is to go against the grain of our mechanical tendencies.

It's more the resistance to unpleasantness,

not just unpleasant thoughts and sensations,

that makes us feel so horrible.

We rarely take a breath without making a judgment.

*Don't mistake **naming** for **knowing**.*

Facing the addiction to worry itself is more useful than resolving the specific content of our worries.

Opposing our thoughts just gives them more attention. The trick is to not push away the thoughts but to not get caught up in them either.

Shame tells us we are worthless at the core. Bringing a merciful awareness from the heart loosens the grip of this pernicious fiction.

What is required to truly open to life is dropping the harshness of the judgmental mind.

Attachment to the **belief** that you can't be happy while in pain may be a greater source of suffering than pain itself.

225

Concentration can silence the world, but true spiritual practice is about opening to life, not shutting it out.

In meditation, the body's position is not nearly as important as whether you're actually present to the physical experience of it.

balance

How can we prioritize equally important but seemingly opposite things? For example, take discipline and effort on the one hand—achieving goals, being productive, making things happen—paired, on the other hand, with letting life be, with just being rather than doing. We obviously need discipline in order to achieve anything of value: education, work, love, health. Yet when discipline takes on a life of its own, striving becomes our mode of being rather than an occasional means of achieving important ends. Coming back to balance requires seeing this addictive striving for what it is—otherwise it will continue to run our life.

Liberation from fear is not about becoming fearless; it's about seeing that fear is not the deepest truth about who we are.

Doubt—the visceral experience of not know-

ing—is one more path to awakening.

Doing battle with yourself is just more useless spinning of the mind.

Perseverance allows us to continue to practice even when practice is not pleasing.

taking pauses

One of the most powerful tools for awakening truth in the midst of your chaotic daily life is to take frequent pauses. Simply stop for a moment and feel what your life is right now. Right now: stop reading and simply experience what this moment feels like.

You can take these pauses any-time throughout the day. Sitting down to meditate is helpful but it's not necessary. Just settle into any moment and simply feel it. With whatever arises—anger, anxiety, rest-lessness—you don't have to "let it go" because, after all, that would just be more doing, more effort. Just let it be there. Remind yourself to **feel this**.

Only when we abandon blame, can we transform the energy of anger into compassionate
service.

two kinds of food

Experiences are like food: they can either nourish you or disrupt your being. Consider anger: when we really pay attention, the arising of anger may feel like a toxin—as if our bodies have ingested something that is making us physically sick. On the other hand, think of something you find calming, like walking in nature or sitting quietly by the ocean. Notice how mind and body usually settle down, as if our being is being nourished by these simple, wholesome experiences. But we can't just walk away from life and leave all the disrupting, unhealthful experiences behind. Instead, we must learn to digest our experiences in a new way: if you welcome a distressing event as an opportunity to awaken, it becomes nourishment instead of poison.

Spiritual practice must address the inevitable clash between what we want and what is.

Conscious suffering leads to conscious understanding.

Contrary to appearance, sexuality is often an area where we don't know what we really think or feel. When unaware, we're most likely to engage in power struggles in the sexual arena that have very little to do with sex itself.

Using relationship to fill the void of longing will only anesthetize it.

One of the most vital things we must all learn is never taught in school: how to be alone with ourselves.

nature

Simple moments of experiencing nature, when we're really present to life, reconnect us with a basic sense of being alive. But you don't have to go to the woods or the ocean to find nature. Nature is not some far-off place; the peace of being in nature is always at hand. It's available even in the midst of a busy city. Feel the air. Hear the sounds. See the colors and shapes. Let all of this replenish your body. Let the world rebalance and nurture your being; recall what it feels like to be reconnected with life.

When we can willingly stay with the experience of fear, without suppressing it, wallowing in it, or judging it, our awareness becomes
a wider container, the stillness, within which
the energy of fear—its thoughts and sensations—can move through us and transform.

The heart that seeks to awaken, to live genuinely, is more real than anything. That nameless drive calls you to be who you most truly are.

Right now, what is your most cherished belief?

the mystery

We think we can experience this world only through our perceptions. We think we see reality, but what we see is our own bubble of perception, filtered through all of our associations and desires, through language and conditioning. As the saying goes, we don't see things as they are, we see them as we are. Yet, awareness is our nature, without bounds, without solidity. We create this bounded world of phenomena in order to survive and make sense of things. Yet when we live only in our bubble of perception, only in the solid world of fixed boundaries, we are cut off from the totality, the mystery of our being.

In spiritual practice, to **know** we don't know and yet keep practicing is the way we go deeper.

We taste the profundity of existence by simultaneously holding both the suffering and the wonder of being alive.

On one level, there is no teacher and no teaching. Ultimately, you must return to your own experience.

*When you really pay attention, **everything** is your teacher.*

who we truly are

When we bring a gentle awareness to the layers of our conditioning, and to the struggles that arise out of our conditioning, the power of that conditioning slowly dissolves. Life then moves toward the unconditioned—where the vastness, or love, just flows through. This is where we can see that we are more than just these thoughts or this body—that this very body-mind **is** the vastness, and simultaneously a unique manifestation of it. As the curtain of separation lifts, we begin to know what life really is. We come to see that the purpose of human life is to become awake to who we truly are—which is the vastness itself, no longer limited to the notion of a separate "self." From this place of connectedness we understand that our deepest wish is to live more openly from the heart; and we also understand that saying yes to life means saying yes to **everything**—even the hard parts.

MORE DAILY WISDOM
365 Buddhist Inspirations
Edited by Josh Bartok
384 pages, ISBN 0-86171-296-X, $16.95

Like its predecessor, *Daily Wisdom, More Daily Wisdom* draws on the richness of Buddhist writings to offer a spiritual cornucopia that will illuminate and inspire day after day, year after year. Sources span a spectrum from ancient sages to modern teachers, from monks to laypeople, from East to West, from poetry to prose. Each page, and each new day, reveals *More Daily Wisdom* carefully selected from the entire list of titles published Wisdom Publications, the premiere publisher of Buddhist books.

Entries included are from some of Buddhism's best-known figures: the Dalai Lama, Sylvia Boorstein, Bhante Gunaratana, Lama Zopa Rinpoche, Lama Yeshe, Bhikkhu Bodhi, and of course, the Buddha and other ancient luminaries. Also included are excerpts from recent Wisdom favorites like *Hardcore Zen, Medicine & Compassion, The Dharma of Star Wars, The Dharma of Dragons and Daemons, Mindfulness Yoga, The Art of Just Sitting,* and many more.

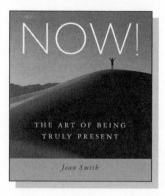

NOW!
The Art of
Being Truly Present
Jean Smith
144 pages,
ISBN 0-86171-480-6, $14.00

"In this timely paperback, the author elucidates the bounties of mindfulness and meditation. On each left-hand page, you will find a brief commentary on a subject that is a natural part of daily living; these are intended to be used pondering, journaling, or discussion in small groups. On the opposite page, you will find invocations [that function as] verses for reflection. These are designed to bring the practice of mindfulness to every moment of existence so that nothing is slighted or overlooked. The book is organized into segments on presence of spirit, of heart, of mind, of conduct, in relationship, and in the world. These reflections and invocations can bring us to a fresh appreciation of being present."—*Spirituality and Health*

wisdom publications

Wisdom Publications, a nonprofit publisher, is dedicated to preserving and transmitting important works from all the major Buddhist traditions as well as exploring related East-West themes.

To learn more about Wisdom, or browse our books on-line, visit our website at wisdompubs.org. You may request a copy of our mail-order catalog on-line or by writing to this address:

WISDOM PUBLICATIONS
199 Elm Street
Somerville, Massachusetts 02144 USA
Telephone: (617) 776-7416
Fax: (617) 776-7841
Email: info@wisdompubs.org
www.wisdompubs.org

THE WISDOM TRUST

As a nonprofit publisher, Wisdom is dedicated to the publication of fine Dharma books for the benefit of all sentient beings and dependent upon the kindness and generosity of sponsors in order to do so. If you would like to make a donation to Wisdom, please do so through our Somerville office. If you would like to sponsor the publication of a book, please write or email us at the address above.

Thank you.

Wisdom is a nonprofit 501(c)(3) organization affiliated with the Foundation for the Preservation of the Mahayana Tradition (FPMT).